THE COLD WAR

HISTORY IN AN HOUR

Also in the *History in an Hour* series

The Cold War

History in an Hour

RUPERT COLLEY

WILLIAM
COLLINS

William Collins
An imprint of HarperCollins*Publishers* Ltd
77–85 Fulham Palace Road
Hammersmith, London W6 8JB
www.harpercollins.co.uk

Visit the History in an Hour website:
www.historyinanhour.com

Published by William Collins in 2013

First published as an eBook by Harper*Press* in 2011

1

A catalogue record for this book
is available from the British Library

ISBN 978-0-00-753915-4

Set in Minion by FMG using Atomik ePublisher from Easypress

Contents

Introduction

From the end of the Second World War to the collapse of the Soviet Union in 1991 the world lived under the shadow of the Cold War. For almost half a century the East and the West eyed each other with suspicion and often hostility. Two ideologies, two political systems, two cultures, two superpowers fought for dominance, each firm in the belief that history would prove them right. And all the time the threat of a Third World War remained a distinct possibility, the spectre of nuclear weapons a constant fear. This, in an hour, is how it happened.

The End of the Second World War: Apocalypse

Winston Churchill, Britain's wartime prime minister, said of Stalin, he would 'work with the Devil if it would help defeat Hitler'. Towards the end of the Second World War, with the defeat of Hitler's Germany only a matter of time, the 'Big Three' – Churchill, Joseph Stalin and the US president, Franklin D. Roosevelt – met a number of times to discuss their strategy for winning the war and the make-up of a post-war Europe. US soldiers, advancing on Berlin from the west, and Soviet soldiers from the east, met on the River Elbe on 25 April 1945. Amidst the handshakes and toasts they promised everlasting friendship between the two nations. But while the soldiers visualized a bright future of camaraderie and peace, the Big Three had already begun carving Europe up between the East and the West.

With the Red Army taking Berlin and indulging in an orgy of mass rape against German women, Hitler, deep within his bunker, committed suicide on 30 April. A week later, on 7 May, Germany surrendered unconditionally. The war – in Europe, at least – was over.

In the Far East, Japan, although on the brink of starvation and collapse, its armed forces shattered, refused to do likewise. The Americans, having successfully tested the first atomic bomb on 16 July, used this new apocalyptic weapon on the Japanese city of Hiroshima on 6 August, followed, three days later, with a second on Nagasaki. Finally, the Japanese surrendered. After six years and a day, the Second World War had ended. And the Cold War began.

The Beginning of the Cold War:
The Freeze

The Big Three talks, the last taking place in Potsdam, west of Berlin, in July 1945, had agreed to split the responsibility for Germany between the Western allies (Britain, the US and France) in western Germany and the Soviet Union in the east. Berlin, one hundred miles within the Soviet hemisphere, would also be split into four zones, one for each of the Allied powers, with a line of communication through eastern Germany to link the western zones of Berlin to western Germany.

It was the attitude of how to treat post-war Germany that illustrated the real differences. The Soviet Union had, both in terms of actual numbers and also proportionately, shed the greatest amount of blood in defeating the Nazis. Therefore Stalin wanted heavy reparations from Germany and for it to be kept economically poor to prevent it rising again as a threat. France, which had been invaded three times by Germany during the previous hundred years, was sympathetic to this view. The Americans, however, felt that an economically strong Germany was vital to the future of Europe, where both capitalism and democracy could flourish so the country would not descend again into a breeding ground for extremism. It had been precisely the period of economic and political chaos in post-First World War Germany that had given Hitler and the Nazis the opportunity to exploit people's dissatisfaction and gain power.

Three Speeches:
'An iron curtain has descended'

In eastern Europe Stalin spread his influence to set up communist governments, where hardline communists loyal to Stalin used intimidation, violence and threats to disrupt the democratic process and seize control. In doing so the east European satellites provided the Soviet Union with a buffer against western Europe. Capitalism, according to a speech Stalin gave in February 1946, made war inevitable; only communism could bring genuine world peace. And as the capitalist nations squabbled among themselves, he continued, the people of western Europe would choose communism.

Churchill, now no longer in office, gave a speech in Missouri on 5 March 1946, in which he coined the phrase the 'Iron Curtain', saying: 'From Stettin in the Baltic to Trieste in the Adriatic, an iron curtain has descended across the continent.' Britain, struggling economically, began the process of dismantling its empire – granting

India independence in 1947, and removing military assistance and economic aid to Greece. The Greeks were in the midst of a bitter civil war between nationalists and communists and the US feared that without British aid, Greece would fall to communism and other struggling European nations would follow.

'The seeds of totalitarian regimes,' said US president, Harry S. Truman, on 12 March 1947, 'are nurtured by misery and want.' In other words, communism appealed to those suffering from hardship; remove the hardship and you remove the appeal of communism. In a speech known as the Truman Doctrine, the president said that communism had to be contained, and that the USA could not, as it did after the First World War, turn its back on Europe – isolationism was no longer an option. Japan's attack on Pearl Harbor in December 1941, which brought the US into the war, was proof that physical distance was no longer a guarantee of safety. In the post-war era a stable Europe was necessary for the future of the 'free world'. Out of fear of communism, the US decided to send aid to Greece.

The Marshall Plan: 'Communism cannot be stopped in Europe'

Three months after Truman's speech, the offer of US aid was extended to any European nation that needed it. This aid package, the European Recovery Program, more commonly known as the Marshall Plan after its originator George C. Marshall, aimed to revive Europe's post-war economies, to alleviate hardship, and to deprive communism of its foothold. Once these economies were stabilized, the theory went, the US, too, would benefit, as trade between Europe and the US increased.

The offer was extended to the countries of eastern Europe and the Soviet Union itself. The Soviet Union had received huge loans from the US during the war to help defeat Germany and now, during the immediate post-war years, further aid would have been hugely beneficial to a country still suffering economically from the consequences of its war effort. But Stalin was never going to allow US/capitalist interference within the Soviet economy, and nor would he permit it in his satellite states. However, Poland and Czechoslovakia, the latter at this stage still a democracy, saw the obvious benefits of US aid, and both accepted invitations to attend a conference in Paris, set for July 1947, to discuss the Marshall Plan. Furious, Stalin forbade them to go. Meekly, representatives of the Polish and Czechoslovakian governments traipsed to Moscow to face their dressing-down from Stalin, and returned home to politely decline the invitation to Paris. By February the following year, Czechoslovakia's communists had staged a coup overthrowing the only democratic government in eastern Europe, replacing it with a communist regime loyal to Stalin and Moscow.

In April 1948, Italy went to the polls. The US Congress was worried: 'If Italy goes red, communism cannot be stopped in Europe', and threatened to prohibit Italy from receiving Marshall aid if the communists won. They did not. The Marshall Plan, therefore, had the effect of reaffirming Churchill's concept of the Iron Curtain by forcing countries to decide whether their loyalties lay to the west or the east. Sixteen countries finally accepted aid, which, by 1952, had amounted to $13 billion. For those who chose the west, Italy and Denmark for instance, economic assistance came hand in hand with military protection with, in April 1949, the formation of NATO (the North Atlantic Treaty Organization), initially signed by twelve countries. West Germany joined in 1955, the same year that the Soviet Union and her seven satellites, as a direct counterbalance to NATO, formed the Warsaw Pact.

Berlin: 'You should not and cannot abandon this city and this people'

The Marshall Plan also contributed to the unravelling of the fragile co-existence between East and West Berlin. In June 1948, the US and Britain announced proposals for establishing the new country of West Germany, and on 23 June introduced a new currency, the Deutschmark, into West Berlin. This immediately caused economic chaos in the Soviet sector as people clamoured to exchange their old money for the new currency. The Soviets responded on 24 June by cutting off all road, rail and canal links between West Germany and West Berlin. The Berlin Blockade had begun. 'People of this world,' said the mayor of West Berlin, 'look upon this city and see that you should not and cannot abandon this city and this people.'

If Stalin's aim was to force the Western powers out of Berlin, it backfired. During the 323 days of the Berlin Airlift, US and British planes supplied West Berlin with 1.5 million tons of supplies, a plane landing every three minutes. Three years earlier, the Allies had been dropping bombs over Berlin; now, the West Berliners joked, they were dropping potatoes. On 12 May 1949, Stalin, knowing he couldn't risk shooting down the planes, and realizing the PR disaster he'd caused, lifted the blockade.

The political division of Germany became official on 23 May 1949 with the formal proclamation in Bonn of the 'Federal Republic of Germany' (West Germany). Five months later, in response, came the proclamation of East Germany with its somewhat misleading title, the 'German Democratic Republic'.

The Bomb: 'MAD'

On 29 August 1949, in the Kazakhstan desert, Soviet scientists, under the leadership of Lavrenti Beria, Stalin's chief of secret police, successfully detonated their first atomic bomb, four years after the bombing of Hiroshima and Nagasaki. When the Americans found out they were shocked – they had anticipated that it would take the Soviets until at least 1953 to reach that stage. Armed with information gleaned from spies working within the US atomic industry and with the use of forced labour, the Soviet Union had broken the US's monopoly. The US then upped the stakes by developing the hydrogen bomb, despite fears that such bombs threatened the very existence of life on earth. But the possibility that the Soviets would develop their own 'superbomb' forced the US hand, and on 1 November 1952, on a tiny Pacific island, the US tested the world's first hydrogen bomb, 1,000 times more powerful than the atomic bomb dropped on Hiroshima.

Less than a year later, on 12 August 1953, the Soviets did indeed test their own H-bomb. The race continued. In March 1954 the Americans detonated a lithium-based hydrogen bomb, the fallout spattering a Japanese fishing boat, the *Lucky Dragon*, eighty-two miles away. The unlucky crew members fell ill, one eventually dying. In October 1961 the Soviet Union successfully tested the world's largest bomb – a single explosion ten times greater than the combined power of all explosives used throughout the Second World War.

The US, concerned over a perceived 'missile gap', increasingly used spy planes over Russia to gather information about the strength of the Soviet nuclear capacity. Khrushchev was furious about these intrusions over Soviet airspace but the US U-2s were able to fly at too high an altitude to be brought down. However, in May 1960, days before a four-power summit in Paris, a Soviet fighter plane did finally bring down a U-2. At first Eisenhower insisted it was not a spy plane but a weather plane. But when Khrushchev provided firm evidence, Eisenhower had to confess. Khrushchev then boycotted the Paris talks and relations between the superpowers deteriorated. The U-2 pilot, Gary Powers, was sentenced to ten years' imprisonment but released after two in exchange for a Soviet spy in US captivity.

The superpowers knew that these bombs could not be used against each other – by doing so they would destroy each other and would make the world uninhabitable. To the end of the Cold War the very existence of humanity lay in this fragile balance of deterrence, known as Mutually Assured Destruction or, rather aptly, MAD. The time had come to discuss how to slow down the arms race, and the first of many, rather meaningless, agreements came in 1963 with the signing of the Limited Test Ban Treaty.

The Korean War: Hot War

The first major conflict – the first 'hot war' of the Cold War – took place in Korea between 1950 and 1953. Ruled by Japan since 1910, Korea rejoiced in Japan's defeat, and, following the end of the Second World War, was split between Soviet and US spheres of influence at the 38th parallel line of latitude into North and South Korea respectively. In 1948 the newly formed United Nations called for free elections in both the North and the South. The Soviets refused to comply and proclaimed the Democratic People's Republic of Korea with Kim Il Sung as its chairman. Elections did take place in the South, although they were boycotted by the communists, and Syngman Rhee was elected president of the Republic of Korea.

Kim Il Sung sought Stalin's permission to invade South Korea and reunify the peninsula. Stalin, fearful of provoking the US, refused. But then two events changed his mind. First, the Soviet Union had developed the atomic bomb. Second came the triumph of communism in China, following a protracted civil war, and the proclamation of the People's Republic of China in October 1949. 'The Chinese people have now stood up!' declared Mao Zedong. Both these events, Stalin felt sure, would make America think twice before going to war over a relatively minor issue such as Korea. With Stalin's authority, on 25 June 1950, Kim Il Sung ordered his army across the 38th parallel into South Korea, taking Seoul three days later. Stalin was wrong in his assessment of the US's reaction. The US moved its army of occupation stationed in Japan into the conflict, executing a counterattack on the port of Inchon in the North and recapturing Seoul on 25 September. The US forces then pushed north, taking the North Korean capital, Pyongyang, on 19 October.

Mao, keen to show his loyalty to Stalin, offered to help. Accordingly, China entered the fray, pushing back the US advance, recapturing the capitals of both North and South Korea, although, in reply, the Americans retook Seoul in March 1951. The conflict now disintegrated into a stalemate of trench warfare. It suited Stalin to keep the war going, if merely to tie the US down in East Asia. Soon after Stalin's death in March 1953 a ceasefire was announced and the war finally ended on 27 July with the boundary between North and South Korea at much the same place as three years and 3 million casualties earlier.

US Anti-Communism:
'Reds Under the Bed'

Following the realization that US spies working for the Soviet Union had accelerated Russia's development of the atomic bomb, anti-communist hysteria swept through 1950s America. In 1953, a married couple, the Rosenbergs, were sent to the electric chair for passing atomic secrets to the Soviets. A series of witch-hunts, orchestrated by Republican senator, Joseph McCarthy, targeted Hollywood, universities and even the originator of the Marshall Plan, George C. Marshall. Richard Nixon, then a congressman, unmasked communist agent Alger Hiss, a former insider in Roosevelt's government, who served forty-four months in prison as a result. In an atmosphere reminiscent of Soviet Russia, people were encouraged to inform on each other and to maintain vigilance against the internal enemy.

Stalin's Final Years:
'I'm finished, I don't even trust myself'

In Russia itself, Stalin, paranoid about everyone, including his own bodyguards, unleashed a new reign of terror, as lethal as the 'Great Terror' of the 1930s, and based on his fears of a Zionist conspiracy, anti-semitic in nature. Every Soviet citizen lived under the cloud of possible arrest and subsequent deportation or execution. Stalin's control over his satellites remained absolute; no socialist state could make any decision or exert any form of independence from Moscow, with the exception of Tito, popular leader of communist Yugoslavia, who placed national autonomy above ideological brotherhood and who, unlike other eastern European leaders, did not need Stalin to keep him in power. Having expelled Tito from Cominform, an alliance of communist leaders set up by Moscow in 1947, Stalin considered invading Yugoslavia to teach Tito a lesson. Ultimately he decided against it.

By the end Stalin trusted no one and suspected everyone,

including his personal doctors most of whom he had arrested. 'I'm finished,' he said in his final days. 'I don't even trust myself.' With the new terror reaching fever pitch, Stalin suffered a stroke and was left to fester for several days, his personal staff too frightened to check on him. He died eventually on 5 March 1953, aged seventy-three.

Despite his tyranny, Stalin's death was received with a public outpouring of grief. His body lay in state and such was the mass of mourners scrabbling to pay their last respects that several people died in the crush. Immediately, the Kremlin started adopting a softer approach, issuing amnesties to many languishing in Stalin's gulags and aborting the campaign of terror. But who, after thirty years, could take the Great Leader's place? Lavrenti Beria, Stalin's chief of secret police since 1938, looked an obvious choice but his detractors within the Soviet hierarchy, fearful of a continuation of Stalin's harsh rule, had Beria arrested on trumped-up charges of espionage, tried him and had him shot. A fate that Beria himself had inflicted on countless thousands of his fellow citizens. As Stalin had said, 'No man, no problem.' It was to be the only issue decided in blood. Nikita Khrushchev then emerged as the new leader. A Ukrainian peasant by origin, impulsive, rotund, by turns vindictive and charming, he represented a more humane version of socialism and offered a different type of leadership from that of his predecessor.

Khrushchev:
'Different roads to socialism'

However, if the East German workers thought Stalin's death meant change, they were soon disabused of this idea, as the Stalinist leader, Walter Ulbricht, strove to increase industrial output. On 16 June 1953, workers in East Berlin went on strike. The strike soon spread to other cities and Soviet tanks had to intervene to quash the uprising. The human face of socialism only went so far.

On 25 February 1956, at the Soviet Twentieth Party Congress, Khrushchev delivered a four-hour speech to party leaders in which he denounced Stalin's methods, acknowledged his mistakes and criticized his murderous reign. He talked also of allowing the Soviet satellites to follow 'different roads to socialism'. The text of the speech, although secret, soon spread across Russia and abroad, causing shock that the great man's name should be so besmirched but also relief that, through Khrushchev's 'de-Stalinization', the tyranny that had overshadowed the Soviet Union for so long was now something of the past. When, eight years later in 1964, Khrushchev himself was deposed and pensioned off, he said: 'I'm glad that the party has gotten to the point when it can rein in even its first secretary.'

In June 1956, in Poland, in a repeat of the East Berlin uprising of 1953, the workers revolted, demanding economic reform. The Polish government, in a conciliatory gesture, replaced their hard-line leader with the popular and reformist Władysław Gomułka. The Poles had taken Khrushchev at his word and were following a 'different road to socialism'. But Khrushchev was not impressed. Furious, he flew unannounced to Warsaw for a showdown with the Poles. Gomułka held his ground but promised that Poland would remain loyal to Moscow. Satisfied with this, Khrushchev withdrew.

But it was the Hungarian Uprising in October 1956 that truly tested the extent of the Soviet Union's resolve. Following the relative success in Poland, students and workers took to the streets, tearing down a huge statue of Stalin, and demanding greater freedom and the right to worship and protesting against the excesses of the Hungarian secret police. Khrushchev ordered in Soviet troops but replaced the unpopular Hungarian leader with the reformist Imre Nagy. With Nagy in place, Khrushchev withdrew his troops to the Hungarian border.

The protest continued and hundreds of Hungary's secret police were lynched. Nagy, siding with the rebels, demanded Hungary's withdrawal from the Warsaw Pact and was prepared to declare Hungary's neutrality. This went much further than Poland; Nagy had gone too far. The rebels hoped and expected support and aid from the West, but Britain and France were distracted by the emerging crisis over the Suez Canal, and the USA by presidential elections. The aid never materialized. Chairman Mao encouraged Khrushchev to take a firmer line, so Khrushchev, taking advantage of the West's preoccupations, ordered the tanks back in. This time, with brutal efficiency, the uprising was crushed.

Nagy sought sanctuary in the Yugoslavian embassy and was replaced by the hardline Janos Kadar, who, loyal to Moscow, remained in charge until 1988. Over 200,000 Hungarians fled across the border into Austria and the West until that escape route was sealed off. Thousands were executed by the regime in reprisal; and Nagy, lured out of the embassy, was arrested, tried and shot. Khrushchev may have denounced Stalin as a tyrant, but when need be, he could be equally ruthless.

Space Wars: 'Flopnik'

Supremacy in space, so the superpowers believed, equated to control of the Earth. On 5 October 1957, the Soviets launched the first satellite, or Sputnik, into space, followed a month later, on 3 November, the fortieth anniversary of the Russian Revolution, with a second, this time with an astronaut of sorts on board – Laika, a dog. Animal lovers throughout the world protested. The Americans were shocked by how far the Soviets had raced ahead, and more so when their own launch, on 6 December, resulted in a humiliating failure when their rocket exploded on take-off: 'Flopnik', teased the press. The US felt it was fast becoming a 'second-rate power' behind the Soviet Union. In response, it formed NASA (National Aeronautics and Space Administration) and did finally succeed in launching its own rocket in January 1958. However, the ultimate humiliation came on 12 April 1961, when the Soviet cosmonaut, Yuri Gagarin, became the first man in space in a round-the-world flight lasting an hour and forty-eight minutes. Gagarin returned a hero and Khrushchev was delighted. The two men toured around Moscow in an open-top car. Stung into action, John F. Kennedy, elected US president in November 1960, promised that America would put the first man on the moon before the end of the decade.

The Berlin Wall:
'Berlin is the testicles of the West'

Stalin very rarely left the confines of the Kremlin. Khrushchev, on the other hand, loved to be seen in public at home and abroad. In September 1959, he visited the USA, met with President Eisenhower and travelled the country, exclaiming with delight at what he saw and arguing in equal measure. 'It is true that for the time being you are richer than we,' he told Eisenhower. 'But we want to be as rich tomorrow as you are now, and richer still the day after.' Khrushchev still believed in the Marxist theory that capitalism would one day fail and communism would be the answer. But as cosmetically successful as the trip may have been, the strained relationship between the superpowers remained.

'Berlin is the testicles of the West,' said Khrushchev; 'every time I want the West to scream, I squeeze on Berlin.' By the early 1960s the difference between West and East Berlin had become marked, the former enjoying prosperity and freedom that made the latter seem drab in comparison. The huge migration from East to West Berlin, and then into West Germany, was a great advertisement for capitalism and an equally poor one for communism and for Ulbricht and Khrushchev. Proposals for a wall to stem the flow were firmly rejected by Moscow – it would only highlight their failure. Better to win the hearts of the East Berliners. But by 1961 almost 3 million mainly young East Germans had gone west, a whole sixth of the population, from communism to capitalism in minutes, causing severe labour shortages and an acute embarrassment for the socialist utopia. Their hearts had not been won. In a meeting between Khrushchev and Kennedy in Vienna, Khrushchev demanded the US's withdrawal from Berlin. It would have meant the city falling entirely under communist control. When Kennedy refused, Khrushchev banged on the table, shouting: 'I want peace but if you want war that's your problem.'

Eventually, on the night of 12–13 August 1961, a barbed-wire fence was erected. As the wire went up, many East Germans made a last-minute dash for freedom among scenes of high tension. Days later, a concrete wall completely encircled the 103-mile perimeter of West Berlin. The most potent symbol of the Cold War was in place.

A border dispute at the wall on 27 October resulted in Soviet and US tanks facing each other 'nose to nose' at Checkpoint Charlie. With instructions coming in from Washington and Moscow, the tanks waited on high alert, ready to open fire if necessary. Finally, after a sixteen-hour stand-off, the first Soviet tank withdrew five yards. A US tank then retreated the same distance, and the confrontation resolved itself.

In June 1963, Kennedy visited West Berlin and, having inspected the wall, addressed a huge crowd in a square that would be renamed in his honour, saying, 'All free men, wherever they may live, are citizens of Berlin, and, therefore, as a free man, I take pride in the words, *Ich bin ein Berliner!*' (A 'Berliner' is also a type of doughnut, so for many it sounded as if Kennedy was saying he was one.) Nonetheless, the speech was a great morale booster for the encircled West Berliners and evidence of the US's solidarity with their plight.

During the twenty-eight years of the wall's existence, numerous attempts were made to escape from East to West Berlin. Many were successful, using ingenious methods as security at the wall tightened. But about 130 people lost their lives in trying to escape to freedom.

The Cuban Missile Crisis: 'We'll all meet together in Hell'

The Cuban Missile Crisis of 1962 epitomized the Cold War as the two superpowers brought the world to the brink of nuclear war. In January 1959, after a two-year guerrilla campaign, Fidel Castro, a Marxist, aided by the charismatic Che Guevara, disposed of Cuban dictator Fulgencio Batista. Khrushchev was delighted that a communist coup had taken place without Soviet encouragement (or bullying).

When Castro nationalized US assets in Cuba, the USA responded by placing a trade embargo on Cuba. The Soviet Union came to Cuba's rescue and the two nations bonded, Castro aligning Cuba to the Soviet cause. When they met at the UN in September 1960 Khrushchev and Castro embraced. The USA, alarmed by this communist presence in their backyard, resolved to have Castro removed from power. In April 1961 a US-backed band of Cuban exiles landed at the Bay of Pigs hoping to raise a counter-uprising against Castro. The invasion failed, Kennedy was heavily criticized, and internal support for Castro deepened as Cuba became firmly anti-American.

Khrushchev decided to use his new ally. In retaliation for the USA aiming missiles at Russia from bases in Turkey, Khrushchev sought Castro's permission to place nuclear missiles in Cuba to face the USA. Castro gave his support and in September 1962 the first installations were in place. Photographs from a US U-2 spy plane exposed the missile sites, sending Washington into a panic. Direct intervention, although favoured by the military and discussed in detail, was discarded for fear of escalating the crisis into war. Instead, Kennedy's administration decided on a naval blockade of Cuba to prevent the arrival of further Soviet ships carrying missiles. The US army and its nuclear weapons were put on red alert and Kennedy addressed the nation on TV.

Khrushchev warned Kennedy against the blockade, threatening the use of submarines against US ships. If it came to nuclear war, Khrushchev warned: 'We'll all meet together in Hell.' By the end of October the American public felt it was on the eve of Armageddon. After intense talks between Moscow and Washington, Khrushchev ordered the withdrawal of the Soviet missiles in return for the withdrawal of the US missiles in Turkey and a US pledge not to attempt an overthrow of Castro. Despite this latter condition, Castro was furious at what he saw as Khrushchev's climb-down. However, the world at least had been saved from devastation.

The Vietnam War: Unwinnable

Indochina was part of France's colonial empire but the Vietnamese defeat of French forces in 1954 led to the Geneva Accords, which recognized the three separate countries of Laos, Cambodia and Vietnam. The latter was to be divided, temporarily, between North and South at the 17th parallel line of latitude, pending elections. North Vietnam was ruled by the communists, under Ho Chi Minh, and the Republic of Vietnam in the south by Ngo Dinh Diem, backed by the USA. Eisenhower feared if Indochina fell to communism, the whole of South-east Asia could fall, the 'domino effect', as he called it.

In North Vietnam the Viet Cong, communist guerrillas, redistributed land to the peasants, evicting and brutalizing the landlords, many of whom fled to the South. Kennedy sent military advisers to South Vietnam but soon decided that Diem, a Catholic whose religious intolerance of Buddhism led many monks to self-immolate in protest, had to be removed. On 2 November 1963, a coup ousted Diem, who was captured and killed. Three weeks later, in Dallas, Kennedy was also assassinated.

In August 1964 a skirmish in the Gulf of Tonkin between the North Vietnamese and US ships gave Kennedy's successor, Lyndon B. Johnson, the pretext to bomb Hanoi and North Vietnam. Over the coming decade the USA were to drop more bombs in Vietnam than by all participants during the whole of the Second World War. US planes dropped the deadly napalm and also herbicides to denude the forests used by the Viet Cong to hide and launch guerrilla attacks. US troops deployed 'search and destroy' missions against the Viet Cong. But nervous and inexperienced US troops, unable to differentiate between enemy and civilian, killed too many innocents. As the bombings intensified, the North received military aid from both the Soviet Union and China.

In January 1968, North Vietnam launched its Tet Offensive, which destroyed many South Vietnamese cities and captured several US targets, including, most alarmingly for Washington, the US embassy in Saigon. By now the war was seen as unjust and 'unwinnable', as the financial costs, which were damaging social reform programmes at home, and casualty rates escalated. In March 1968 Johnson, increasingly unpopular and unable to find a way out without the USA losing face, declared he wouldn't be standing for re-election later that year.

Rebellion: 1968

As peace talks between the North and South Vietnamese failed, the US draft was extended, resulting in anti-war protests across the USA. The hippy scene gathered steam as American youth embraced 'flower power', frequently clashing with the police, and culminating in the shooting of demonstrators at the Democratic Party convention in Chicago in August 1968. Race riots took place as the civil rights movement gained momentum, the lowest point being the shooting of Martin Luther King in April 1968. With the assassination two months later of Democrat presidential hopeful, Robert Kennedy, the nation seemed to be in chaos.

In Europe too there were demonstrations and riots in London and Paris. In Britain the growing strength of CND (Campaign for Nuclear Disarmament) and the annual marches to Britain's primary nuclear base at Aldermaston alarmed the government. In the Soviet Union life was typified by economic stagnation, overcrowding and long queues for the most basic of commodities. Khrushchev's attempts at introducing new initiatives, such as harvesting grain in Central Asia, backfired despite some initial success, leaving whole tracts of land useless. This was also the time of softening up, when Khrushchev released from the gulags prominent political prisoners, including Aleksandr Solzhenitsyn who was allowed to publish his books, including *One Day in the Life of Ivan Denisovich*. Soviet youth, known as *beatniki*, listened to Western music, especially The Beatles, and painted and wrote as they saw fit. But it was during a visit to an exhibition of avant-garde art that Khrushchev brought this relative freedom to an abrupt end. Dismayed at what the Soviet youth was producing he ordered an immediate clampdown and a return to firm party discipline.

In January 1968 in Czechoslovakia, amidst growing discontent at economic failure, the Communist Party appointed Alexander Dubček as chairman. Dubček promised reform, democratization and 'socialism with a human face'. Having begun the process, the 'Prague Spring', Moscow feared he had gone too far and ordered Dubček to rein in his 'counter-revolutionary' methods. His failure to bring Czechoslovakia back in line angered the Soviet Union's new leader, Leonid Brezhnev, who, on 20 August, with support from other Warsaw Pact leaders, ordered in the tanks. Dubček, rendered powerless, was arrested and later exiled to a minor post, and replaced by a hardliner, loyal to Moscow. Czechoslovakia's Prague Spring was over. Brezhnev, in a speech in November 1968, reiterated the right of the Warsaw Pact to intervene if any Soviet satellite compromised the hegemony of the Eastern Bloc by looking west. Known as the 'Brezhnev Doctrine', it ushered in another period of suppression, the straitjacketing of the arts and ideological strictness.

Nixon: 'Vietnamization'

Following the US elections in November 1968, Richard Nixon, the new Republican president, promised to 'bring us together', and pledged the gradual withdrawal of troops from Vietnam. The war, however, continued and Nixon ordered the bombing of Cambodia from where the supply of arms was reaching the North Vietnamese, while telling the American public that the USA respected Cambodia's neutrality. Slowly, Nixon managed to hand back the organization of the day-to-day military operations to the South Vietnamese in what he called 'Vietnamization'.

The Paris Accords of January 1973 finally brought a ceasefire in Vietnam but allowed the Viet Cong to maintain the territory already captured in South Vietnam, much to the displeasure of the South Vietnamese. Although the last US soldiers had left Vietnam by the end of March, the USA continued to supply arms to the South while the Soviets continued to supply the North. As

Nixon began withdrawing aid, the North gained the upper hand, eventually defeating South Vietnam in 1975, resulting in the panicked evacuation of the South Vietnamese 'boat people'. Communist armies also triumphed in Laos and Cambodia. Eisenhower's great fear had come to pass and the whole of Indochina was now communist.

China, the USA and the Soviet Union: 'Ping-pong diplomacy'

Relations between the new communist China and the Soviet Union began promisingly with the signing of the Sino-Soviet Treaty in 1950. But the relationship began deteriorating following Khrushchev's speech in 1956 denouncing Stalin and his reign of terror. In 1958 Chairman Mao launched the Great Leap Forward: a massive drive to increase industrial output to match and exceed that of the West. He ordered farmers to build furnaces and make steel to the detriment of agriculture. The result was catastrophic with over 30 million dying from hunger, history's worst ever famine, the responsibility for which lay not with nature but a single man.

Mao saw himself as the leader of world communism and he viewed with growing disdain what he saw as the Soviet Union's co-existence with the USA, confirmed for him by Khrushchev's visit to the USA in 1959. Khrushchev's subsequent visit to China did not go well and Mao felt slighted that the Soviet leader had gone to the USA first. Khrushchev's withdrawal of missiles from Cuba was, to Mao, further evidence of his weakness. In turn, the Soviet Union withdrew its aid to China, including support for its development of the atomic bomb. But even without the Soviet Union's support, China successfully tested its first bomb in 1964 and, three years later, the hydrogen bomb. By 1969, border disputes between the two communist superpowers led to fighting and risked escalating into full-scale and possibly nuclear war.

In 1966, Mao, fearing China's revolutionary spirit was, like the Soviet Union's during Khrushchev's reign, slackening, launched the Cultural Revolution. Militant Chinese youth, the 'Red Guard', brandishing Mao's Pocket Book, ran amok throughout the country destroying anything they considered old and bourgeois, including much of China's ancient heritage, and terrorizing and killing anyone they deemed counter-revolutionary. Mao, having watched his Red Guards wreak chaos across the country and kill over half a million people, reined in their excesses and sent them out to work on farm collectives to be 're-educated'.

The USA, keen to exploit the rift between China and the Soviet Union, made increasingly friendly overtures to the People's Republic of China. In 1971, an accidental meeting of the US and Chinese table tennis teams resulted, with Mao's permission, in a championship won convincingly by the Chinese team. From this 'ping-pong diplomacy' great advances were made. China was admitted into the UN, the USA ended a twenty-one-year trade embargo on China, and Secretary of State Henry Kissinger's secret visit to China in 1971 paved the way for President Nixon's official visit in February 1972, where, among handshakes, toasts and photo opportunities, Mao and Nixon, both concerned about the threat posed by the Soviet Union, found a meeting of minds.

Meanwhile, the Soviet Union's own improvement of relations

with the USA made slow progress. The Strategic Arms Limitation Talks of 1969–72 (SALT I) brought much agreement on the deployment and potential uses of nuclear missiles, together with the signing of the 'Basic Principles', which called for peaceful co-existence between the two superpowers. In 1972, Nixon visited Moscow and the following year Brezhnev visited the USA. The Cold War had entered the era of détente.

But the Nixon presidency came to a premature end when a bungled burglary at the Democratic Party's HQ in Washington DC started a trail that led right to the White House and the heart of government. Nixon's attempt to cover up his involvement only led to his downfall. Public opinion put legality above state brinkmanship and in August 1974 Nixon resigned, the only president in US history to do so, to be replaced by Gerald Ford.

The post-war boundaries in eastern Europe had never been officially recognized. In 1969, in a policy named *Ostpolitik*, Willy Brandt, West Germany's chancellor, formally accepted East Germany as a state, and in 1970 signed non-aggression pacts with the Soviet Union and Poland. It meant Germany had finally recognised and accepted the post-war boundaries between Germany and Poland imposed at the 1945 Potsdam Conference. In a symbolic visit to Warsaw, Brandt knelt at the memorial to the Warsaw Ghetto and expressed sorrow for Nazi crimes in Poland.

In 1975, détente reached its high mark with the signing of the Helsinki Accords between the USA and the Soviet Union, together with thirty-three other countries. In the skies above, an American and a Soviet spacecraft symbolically docked together. Helsinki was a triumph for the Soviet Union, for the Accords recognized the existing borders within eastern Europe, an objective the Soviet Union had sought since the end of the war in 1945. But the payback, for Brezhnev, was the agreement to respect human rights and to allow freedom of movement within Europe.

The Decline of Détente:
'Lennonism, not Leninism'

The Soviet Union had no intention of respecting the human rights conditions and when dissidents tried to remind Brezhnev and the Politburo of their Helsinki obligations they were swiftly dealt with and either exiled or declared insane and locked away. The ringleaders of a Czech dissident group, Charter 77, including the future president of the Czech Republic, the playwright, Václav Havel, were imprisoned. A fan of The Beatles, Havel was said to be not so much a Leninist as a Lennonist. The freedom of movement clause was also blatantly ignored while Western protests were brushed aside.

SALT I also began to unravel. The agreement, signed in 1972, allowed for the modernization of existing weapons, a clause which both the USA and the Soviet Union exploited, subtly at first, then increasingly less so. More talks were needed. The SALT II discussions began in 1977, but even while talks were under way the Soviet Union increased spending on nuclear armament, while the Americans began placing short-range missiles in Europe, despite strong opposition, most notoriously from the women of Greenham Common in Berkshire in England. Nonetheless, SALT II was signed two years later in June 1979, but by then relations between the superpowers were at such a low ebb that the treaty was never ratified.

Situations in other parts of the world also helped unravel the spirit of détente. The countries of the Middle East were allying themselves to one or the other of the superpowers. In Egypt, Anwar al-Sadat looked to his sponsor, the Soviet Union, to retrieve Arab territory lost to Israel during the Six-Day War of 1967. But the Soviets were unwilling to be drawn further into Middle Eastern tensions.

Frustrated by the lack of Soviet assistance, Sadat launched a surprise attack on Israel. The day was 6 October 1973, the Jewish Day of Atonement or 'Yom Kippur'. The joint Egyptian and Syrian attack made initial headway, but the Israelis regrouped and fought back. The USA and the Soviet Union supplied arms and aid to the Israelis and the Arabs respectively while trying to negotiate a ceasefire. The ceasefire came about at the end of October after Nixon had placed his forces on full nuclear alert. The superpowers had failed to work together, reverting back to supporting opposing sides and bringing into question their commitment to détente. Following the Yom Kippur War the Arabs, resentful of American aid to Israel to the tune of $2 billion, restricted the supply of oil, causing price increases and economic chaos in the West.

In 1977 Sadat visited Israel and held talks with the Israeli prime minister, Menachem Begin, during which Sadat formally recognized the state of Israel and managed to retrieve some of the Arab territory lost to Israel in 1967. The Camp David talks, mediated by the new US president, Jimmy Carter, had no room for the Soviets, who felt angered by their isolation. This further damaged détente. Sadat and Begin jointly won the Nobel Peace Prize but their harmony upset Arab nationalists and on 6 October 1981 Sadat was assassinated.

In 1970 the world's first freely elected Marxist government came to power in Chile with Salvador Allende as president. Alarmed by this development, the USA officially stopped aid to Chile and, unofficially, the CIA organized a series of covert operations intended to undermine Allende's power. The economy stagnated and, as planned by the USA, unrest paralysed the country. In September 1973 General Augusto Pinochet seized power in a coup. Allende was killed and Pinochet, ruling as a dictator, ordered the execution of Allende's supporters, many of whom were rounded up in football stadiums and shot. When the CIA's role in bringing down Allende came to light President Ford was heavily criticized for undermining a democratically elected government.

In Iran, the Shah pursued a policy of modernization and Westernization which, although often successful, benefited only the privileged few. The Shah's ruthlessness against the majority of the population prompted no condemnation from the USA, which had brought him to power in 1953 and continued to send him aid and support in return for oil and a fierce anti-communist stance. But in January 1979, with the tide turning against him, the Shah was forced to flee. In his place the Ayatollah Khomeini established Iran as an Islamic republic and denounced the USA as the 'Great Satan'. The Shah's supporters were, like Allende's in Chile, arrested and executed. Islamic (or Sharia) law was introduced and the process of Westernization reversed.

In November 1979, a group of Iranian students kidnapped sixty-six Americans in the US embassy in Tehran. Threats, counter-threats and negotiations all failed and the situation reached stalemate. In April 1980 President Carter sent in US helicopters in a daring rescue mission that failed, humiliating Carter, undermining his position and greatly contributing to his electoral defeat in November that year.

Afghanistan: 'The Soviet Vietnam'

If the USA was facing trouble around the world trying to keep pro-American governments in power, then the Soviet Union was faring little better. In 1978, a pro-Soviet regime took power in Afghanistan and, as in Iran, implemented reforms resented by the Muslim Mujahideen who, funded and supported by the Ayatollah Khomeini, fought against the 'Godless' government. The Soviets sent advisers and aid to help prop up the new regime but in 1979 the Mujahideen, in an attempted coup, killed hundreds of government supporters and several Soviet advisers. The government survived but its president, Nur Mohammad Taraki, sensing the end was near, appealed to the Kremlin for assistance, while his prime minister, Hafizullah Amin, led the reprisals against the rebels, killing thousands, including women and children. The Politburo declined to send help, fearful of the reaction of Soviet Muslims and believing that intervention would only commit the

Soviet Union to a 'Soviet Vietnam'. They advised Taraki to get rid of Amin, with whom splits were emerging. After Taraki returned from Moscow, in September he summoned Amin to the People's Palace. Amin, aware that he was likely to be assassinated, came prepared. A shoot-out ensued; Amin escaped but returned and arrested Taraki, who was later suffocated with a pillow. Amin took power but was distrusted by both the Americans and the Soviets.

The new situation in Afghanistan demanded a rethink within the Kremlin, which concluded that the toppling of a pro-Soviet regime set a bad example which could be repeated elsewhere and that a show of force was needed. They also feared that this new anti-Soviet regime might invite the Americans in, thereby compromising the Afghan buffer zone on the Soviet border. On Christmas Eve 1979, Soviet tanks for the first time invaded the territory of a neutral country. Soviet troops stormed the capital, Kabul, and killed Amin. Carter, in his last days as US president, led the worldwide condemnation of the Soviet invasion. The USA shipped arms to the Muslim rebels, brought a halt to the ratification of the SALT II Treaty, increased military spending and, as a final gesture, announced its boycott of the coming summer Olympics in Moscow, the first to be held within the Eastern Bloc. The British Olympic team, in defiance of Prime Minister Margaret Thatcher, still attended.

The Soviet Union's war against Afghanistan dragged on for nine years and proved to be, exactly as feared by the Politburo, the Soviet Vietnam.

The Polish Pope and Solidarity: 'The last nails in the coffin of communism'

The appointment of Cardinal Karol Wojtyla as Pope John Paul II in October 1978, Poland's first pope and the first non-Italian pope for over 450 years, inspired a country dogged by economic shortages and cultural stagnation. On his first visit home as pope, in June 1979, John Paul II fell to his feet and kissed the ground at Warsaw Airport. Throughout his tour of the country he was enthusiastically greeted with chants of 'We want God, we want God!' When he returned to the Vatican, the pope had left his people with greater courage and a vital sliver of hope.

Price increases in Poland during 1980 led to widespread strikes and the formation of Solidarity, the first independent trade union within the Eastern Bloc. The Polish government, realizing the strength of the movement, allowed its existence and its right to protest if, in return, it recognized the Communist Party and the role of the Soviet Union. The charter was signed by former electrician, Lech Walesa, using a large pen that bore the image of Pope John Paul II.

Centred round the Lenin Shipyards in Gdansk on the Baltic coast, Solidarity demanded better wages, democratic reform and, following the pope's visit, the right to worship. Moscow, by now embroiled in Afghanistan, refused to be drawn in. But over the following year economic hardship in Poland intensified, Solidarity's membership expanded and the threat to the establishment grew more acute. Further strikes in December 1981 led, this time, to a crackdown by the Polish government as tanks appeared on the streets. Martial law was imposed, Solidarity banned and its leaders, including Walesa, arrested and its supporters intimidated. On his arrest, Walesa declared, 'This is the moment of your defeat; you have just put in the last nails in the coffin of communism.' The crackdown had been wholly Polish – the Kremlin had significantly stayed aloof, refusing to intervene as it had done in the past. It was a move away from the Brezhnev Doctrine that insisted on forceful intervention in any attempt to reject socialism within its sphere of influence.

The Ex-Actor: 'Regimes planted by bayonets do not take root'

In January 1981, a few days short of his seventieth birthday, Ronald Reagan became the oldest president in American history. No believer in détente, which he considered a mere continuation of the status quo, Reagan immediately went on the offensive, increasing military spending and calling the Soviet Union an 'evil empire'. He considered negotiations with the Soviet Union a sign of feebleness, and criticized the lack of free elections in eastern Europe: 'Regimes planted by bayonets do not take root.' Reagan initiated a defensive anti-missile system in space, the Strategic Defense Initiative (SDI or, as it was nicknamed, 'Star Wars'). The SDIs could neutralize incoming missiles, while leaving the USA's own offensive missiles free to reach their targets. So, although labelled 'defensive', the Soviet Union regarded SDIs as an offensive development because, in effect, Star Wars destroyed the balance of Mutually Assured Destruction that had kept the superpowers in check for over thirty years.

Unlike his predecessors, containment of communism wasn't enough for Reagan – he wanted to destroy it wherever possible. The 'Reagan Doctrine' provided support for anti-communist fighters throughout the world. He increased military aid to the Afghan rebels still fighting the Soviets. In Nicaragua, the Sandinistas, a left-wing liberation movement backed by Cuba, had in 1979 disposed of the brutal but pro-American regime. Reagan went on the attack against the Sandinistas, providing military assistance to the counter-revolutionaries, the Contras.

In 1983, Reagan sent troops on to the Caribbean island of Grenada, following the assassination of their prime minister, in order to prevent the island from becoming what Reagan called a 'Soviet colony'. Margaret Thatcher protested at the invasion of a Commonwealth country. But, having established a democratically elected regime, the USA withdrew.

On 1 September 1983, a Soviet fighter plane shot down a Korean civilian airliner flying over its airspace, killing the 269 passengers on board, including 63 Americans. Reagan accused the Soviets of terrorism. The delayed response from the Kremlin seemed to confirm their guilt, but the Soviet pilot had followed correct protocol and despite issuing several warnings, including a warning shot, received no response from the airliner. Concluding that it was a spy plane, he followed orders and shot it down. The episode further worsened the poor relations between the superpowers and a few weeks later the Soviets walked out of the next round of arms reduction talks. The Cold War was the coldest it had been for twenty years. When, in November 1983, NATO forces in Europe underwent a nuclear war exercise, the Kremlin genuinely believed the world was on the eve of a Third World War.

That the Soviet leaders should even think along these lines shocked Reagan who, as a result, began talking of meeting the Soviets halfway. He began to see the conflict in terms of the ordinary citizens, 'the Ivan and Anya and the Jim and Sally', who were less concerned with their respective governments and their differing ideologies than their domestic lives, in which they shared common ground. The Soviets, relieved by Reagan's softer approach, suggested a return to the table to discuss arms limitation but nonetheless still boycotted the 1984 Los Angeles Olympics.

Brezhnev had died in November 1982 after eighteen years in charge and was replaced by Yuri Andropov. Andropov himself died in February 1984 and was replaced by 73-year-old Konstantin Chernenko, who died in March 1985. Reagan quipped how could he meet with the Russians if 'they keep dying on me'. But the new man in the Kremlin, Mikhail Gorbachev, was, at fifty-four, the youngest leader in Soviet history.

Gorbachev:
'Mr Gorbachev, tear down this wall!'

'We can't go on living like this,' was Gorbachev's considered summary of life in the Soviet Union during the 1980s. The economy lagged behind that of the West, the people lived in poverty and without hope. The cost of being a superpower was crippling – the commitment to conventional and nuclear arms, the funding of communist regimes elsewhere in the world, and the costly and unpopular war in Afghanistan were all taking their toll on the economy and the everyday lives of Soviet citizens.

Gorbachev introduced the words *perestroika* and *glasnost* into the international arena. The former meaning *reconstruction* (of the Soviet economy and as a nation) and the latter meaning *openness* (a move away from the traditional Soviet model of a closed society with its secret industrial cities and 'cloak and dagger' governance). Gorbachev toured the country, met its workers and crucially, as no Soviet leader had done before, listened. The international community welcomed the appointment of the new man in the Kremlin. Margaret Thatcher, who acted as the intermediary between the superpowers, said of him, 'I like Mr Gorbachev, we can do business together.' Part of the process was to mend the Soviet Union's fractious relationship with the USA. However, what Gorbachev did not want to do was to destroy the Communist Party or the Soviet Union.

Gorbachev and Reagan met several times, the first being at Geneva in November 1985, and despite their ideological and cultural differences, the two men built a rapport that was to have a real and lasting effect on the thawing of the Cold War.

During the course of their meetings, the two leaders talked of the necessity to abandon the arms race, Gorbachev even going so far as to propose an elimination of all nuclear weapons by the year 2000. For Gorbachev this was a necessity; the arms race was costing the Soviet Union dear, money that could be better spent on improving economic conditions at home. Despite their advances, obstacles remained – Reagan wouldn't budge on his Star Wars programme, the SDI. The war in Afghanistan continued, with the USA still supplying arms to the rebels, and at home Gorbachev faced criticism from communist hardliners who felt threatened by his friendship with the American president.

It was Chernobyl that convinced Gorbachev that he was doing the right thing. On 26 April 1986, the nuclear power plant near Kiev in the Ukraine was destroyed by an internal explosion. The radioactive fallout was greater than that caused by the atomic bomb over Hiroshima. The effects were felt as far away as Ireland. The authorities, more concerned with poor publicity than the safety of the local population, took several days to evacuate the area. The health effects, including radiation-related illnesses, are still in evidence today. Chernobyl highlighted the need for reform within the Soviet system and it was a lesson not wasted on Gorbachev.

In June 1987, Reagan visited West Berlin and, like Kennedy a quarter of a century before, inspected the Berlin Wall. 'Mr Gorbachev,' he demanded in a televised speech, 'tear down this wall!'

Finally, after almost nine years, the 'Soviet Vietnam' came to an end. With mounting casualty rates and growing opposition to the war at home, Gorbachev knew that the conflict had become, like Vietnam, unwinnable. Despite the Soviet–Afghanistan cease-fire, both the Soviet Union and the USA continued supplying arms to their factions, ensuring a protracted civil war in Afghanistan. But the expense of maintaining pro-Soviet regimes across the world, including within the Eastern Bloc, and the tremendous cost of the arms race were still crippling the Soviet Union.

On 7 December 1988, Gorbachev delivered a speech to the UN that acted as the starting pistol for tumultuous change in eastern Europe. He talked of nations having the right to a 'freedom of choice' and renounced the Brezhnev Doctrine: 'the threat of force cannot be and should not be an instrument of foreign policy'. As a backup to his words, he promised the withdrawal of troops from the Soviet satellites. But where, the Warsaw Pact leaders wondered, did that leave them, without the support of the Soviet Union?

1989: 'Time to yield power'

The people of the Eastern Bloc who had always hoped for change were now demanding it. They wanted an end to the secret police and its army of informers, the right to worship, the freedom to travel, the right to better economic conditions, to better housing. The right, in short, to a better life.

The first evidence that change was in the air took place in Czechoslovakia with a mass demonstration. The government, acting without Soviet aid, crushed the protest, arresting, among many, Václav Havel. Hungary was the first to take the walk towards freedom, its government allowing the formation of alternative political parties and cutting down the barbed-wire frontier along the Austrian border. June 1989 saw the reburial and state funeral of Imre Nagy, the reformist Hungarian leader, executed on the orders of the Kremlin following the failed Hungarian Uprising thirty-three years before. In October, Gorbachev agreed to withdraw Soviet tanks from the country. Within a year, Hungary held its first round of free elections. In Poland, after a ban of seven years, the government recognized Solidarity. In August 1989, a million protesters formed a human chain 430 miles long linking the three capitals of the Baltic States, Riga, Vilnius and Tallinn.

In May 1989, Gorbachev visited China to improve the still-frosty relations between the two communist superpowers. While the Chinese leaders talked of reform, the youth demanded it, coming out in force on the streets of Beijing, congregating in Tiananmen Square. It was only after Gorbachev's departure that the authorities sent in the tanks and crushed the rebellion with extreme force. But would Gorbachev resort to such measures? His UN speech only six months before implied not.

While China used old-fashioned brutality, the first communist regime fell through the ballot box. Poland's first post-war free elections returned a 99 per cent vote for Solidarity. When the Polish communists rang Moscow for advice, Gorbachev advised that it was time to 'yield power'. On 24 August 1989, the first non-communist government in post-war eastern Europe came into power. Communism in Poland was dead. In July 1989, George Bush, Senior, as the new president, visited Poland and Hungary and praised their first steps towards democracy.

By the autumn of 1989 almost 15,000 East Germans had taken a 'holiday' to Hungary and from there crossed the frontier, now stripped of its barbed wire, into Austria and the West. Other East Germans crammed into the West German embassy in Hungary seeking asylum. In October, the East German government tried to ignore these embarrassments as Gorbachev visited for the regime's fortieth-anniversary celebrations. Erich Honecker, the last of the communist hardliners, raised his glass and talked of East Germany's prosperity. On their official walks the crowd shouted out to Gorbachev, 'Gorby, save us, save us!' In the East German city of Leipzig demonstrators chanted, 'We are the people.' Honecker dismissed Gorbachev's suggestions for reform. Talking to Honecker, Gorbachev said later, was like 'throwing peas against a wall'. In Leipzig, Honecker ordered the police to open fire. But they refused. In the political fallout, Honecker, leader for eighteen years, was forced to resign.

On 4 November, a rock concert designed to support the East German regime became a public platform denigrating the party and demanding not reform but full democracy. On 9 November, Egon Krenz, Honecker's brief successor, announced that, from the following day, East Berliners could apply for visas to visit West Berlin. In itself this was a massive concession but the crowds, already congregating at the wall, asked why wait for visas? The border guards, under immense pressure from the crowds, opened the gates. A trickle stepped tentatively through, followed by more. Soon the trickle had become a torrent. People climbed the wall and began hacking at it as the world watched on television. After twenty-eight years the Berlin Wall, the symbol of the Cold War, had come down.

Within days the dreaded secret police force, the Stasi, was disbanded. Within four months, East Germany held its first free election since 1946. As with forty-five years earlier, the communists were convincingly beaten. This time, however, they were finished. Seven months later, on 3 October 1990, East and West Germany no longer existed. After forty-one years as a country artificially split into two, Germany was a reunified nation.

Following the collapse of the Berlin Wall, events now moved with their own momentum. In Bulgaria, the hardline communists were deposed by reformist communists, who themselves were voted out within a year. In Czechoslovakia, a demonstration on 17 November in Prague's Wenceslas Square was shot upon, but further demonstrations attracted increasingly large numbers. The police couldn't shoot them all. Dubček, the instigator of the Prague Spring twenty-two years before, spoke to the crowds, as did the future president, Václav Havel, recently released from another spell in prison. The 'Velvet Revolution' brought down the government, who, realizing that no help would be forthcoming from Moscow, knew their situation was untenable. Two years later, in 1992, Czechoslovakia, an artificially created country following the First World War, was no more, split into two separate states: the Czech Republic and Slovakia.

In Romania, Nicolae Ceauşescu, president for the previous fifteen years, argued against reform and walked out of talks with Gorbachev and other new enlightened leaders within the Eastern Bloc. Demonstrations broke out across the country, the police shooting several people. On 22 December, Ceauşescu delivered a speech from the balcony of his presidential palace in Bucharest. Designed to garner support for his regime, he had it televised, but the reaction he received was far from what he expected. Booed and heckled, he broke off his speech halfway through, and with his wife and deputy prime minister, Elena, fled by helicopter. Caught three days later, on Christmas Day 1989, the Ceauşescus were put through a brief show trial, then executed. Television footage of their bodies was seen throughout the world.

Only in Yugoslavia was there widespread and protracted violence. Another artificial country thrown together in 1918, Yugoslavia was made up of several republics. Following the Second World War it was held together by the popular Tito. But following Tito's death in May 1980, regional and ethnic rivalries sprang up which, after the disintegration of the Eastern Bloc, led to a vicious civil war which saw ethnic cleansing and genocide, requiring the intervention of UN forces and NATO.

The End of the Soviet Union: 'The threat of a world war is no more'

With eastern Europe now free of communist rule, attention turned to the Soviet Union. In spring 1990, the Baltic states of Lithuania, Estonia and Latvia (unwilling and resentful Soviet satellites since Stalin's annexation at the start of the Second World War) all declared themselves independent. Gorbachev, not wanting to see the break-up of the union, resisted, even cutting gas and oil supplies, but was soon forced to relent. In Russia itself demonstrations in Moscow called for the end of one-party rule. In June 1991, Boris Yeltsin, recently elected mayor of Moscow, was also elected president of the Russian Federation, stating that Russian legality took precedence over the Soviet Union's. Yeltsin was determined to finish off the Communist Party, and with it the Soviet Union.

In July and August, the Soviet republics including the Ukraine, Armenia and Kazakhstan announced their separation from the union. Gorbachev, recently awarded the Nobel Peace Prize and lauded abroad, became under increasing pressure at home. In October, the Soviet Union caved in and allowed its people the freedom to worship and granted the media liberty from state control.

In January 1991, Moscow tried to seize back control of the Baltic states. Fourteen people were killed in Vilnius, the capital of Lithuania, and five more in Riga, the capital of Latvia. Seeing this return to Soviet bullyboy tactics, George Bush Senior protested but was brusquely rebuffed by Moscow. Gorbachev defended the crackdown but, realizing that no one except the Kremlin hardliners would tolerate the continuation of such a policy, called a halt.

In June 1991 the last Soviet tanks left eastern Europe and shortly afterwards the Warsaw Pact was dissolved.

On 19 August 1991, the remaining hardliners within the Kremlin decided that Gorbachev was no longer the man to lead the Communist Party. If they wanted to save both the party and the Soviet Union, it was time to act. Gorbachev, on holiday on the Black Sea, was declared too ill to perform his duties and placed under house arrest. The hardliners imposed emergency rule but their coup lacked the support to succeed. Outside the White House, home to the new Russian parliament, Yeltsin stood on top of a tank declaring the coup illegal and urging people not to support it. The coup duly failed. Gorbachev returned to Moscow hoping to salvage the situation and save the Communist Party just as Yeltsin was dissolving it. On live television Gorbachev and Yeltsin argued, and when Yeltsin exposed members of Gorbachev's government as being behind the coup, Gorbachev, humiliated, was finished.

On 8 December 1991, Yeltsin, on behalf of Russia and with other former Soviet republics, formed the Commonwealth of Independent States, the CIS. The Union of Soviet Socialist Republics had ceased to exist. On Christmas Day the hammer and sickle flag of the Soviet Union was lowered over the Kremlin for the last time as Gorbachev delivered his farewell speech: 'The threat of a world war is no more.'

The Cold War was at an end.

Appendix One: Key Players

Joseph Stalin 1879–1953

Born on 18 December 1878, Josef Vissarionovich Dzhugashvili is better known to history by his adopted name – Stalin, 'man of steel'.

Training to be a priest, Stalin was expelled from his seminary in 1899 and from there followed the revolutionary path of a Marxist.

Following the October Revolution in 1917 and the formation of the Soviet Union, Lenin delegated numerous tasks to his eager protégé, culminating in 1922 with Stalin's appointment as general secretary of the Communist Party. But Lenin began to regret his decision and Stalin's fast-track rise through the party hierarchy, believing Stalin to lack the necessary tact and skill for such a post. In January 1923, Lenin penned a secret memorandum, known as Lenin's Testament, suggesting Stalin's removal from power: 'I am not sure whether [Stalin] will always be capable of using [his] authority with sufficient caution ... Stalin is too rude and this defect ... becomes intolerable in a secretary general. That is why I suggest that the comrades think about a way of removing Stalin from that post and appointing another man in his stead.'

The other man Lenin had in mind was Stalin's great rival, Leon Trotsky. Together with Trotsky, Lenin was going to use the party congress in April that year as his opportunity to have Stalin removed. But in March Lenin suffered a stroke, his third, which confined him to home and effectively ended his political career.

In January 1924 Lenin died. Trotsky may have been the obvious successor but two of his rivals, Lev Kamenev and Grigori Zinoviev, suppressed Lenin's memorandum and decided to side with Stalin, from whom they felt they had nothing to fear. Trotsky was promptly sidelined and eventually expelled from the party and exiled from the country. But if Kamenev and Zinoviev thought they could tame the Georgian beast they were wrong. Stalin sided with Nikolai Bukharin to have them removed from the party before turning on Bukharin as well. Between 1936 and 1938 Kamenev, Zinoviev and Bukharin were all put through show trials accused of ridiculous charges, sentenced and executed.

Stalin's final years were marked by increasing paranoia and obsession about security to the point that he trusted no one, including, as he once said, himself.

In March 1953, Stalin suffered a stroke and, unable to move or call for help, was left unaided, his staff too fearful to disturb him. He died on 3 March, a victim of his own power.

Stalin's body was embalmed and placed next to Lenin's. But in 1961, during the years of de-Stalinization, the body was removed from the Lenin Mausoleum and reburied in a common grave along the Kremlin wall.

Mao Zedong 1893–1976

The son of a wealthy peasant farmer, Mao Zedong (also Mao Tse-Tung) was born in Hunan Province, in south-central China, in 1893. Aged thirteen, he began working on the family farm and was forced into an arranged marriage. He left home to escape his overbearing father and the rigours of rural life. He served briefly in the revolutionary army during the 1911 Chinese Revolution which saw the end of the Qing Dynasty and the formation of the

Chinese republic. As a student he began dabbling in politics, then worked as a library assistant at Peking University, during which time he converted to Marxism.

Mao was an early supporter of the Chinese Communist Party (CCP), established in Shanghai in June 1921.

Having originally turned his back on the rural life, he began to see the future of revolutionary power not in the urban classes but in the countryside. He established various peasant organizations, giving the peasants a political voice.

In 1923, the communists formed an alliance with the Kuomintang (Nationalist Party) and Mao became a member of its Executive Bureau and head of its propaganda arm. But following the death of the Nationalist Party leader, Chiang Kai-Shek was appointed leader of the Kuomintang, and immediately began purging the party of its communist element. Its survivors were forced to relocate in what became known as the Long March, with Mao leading 100,000 followers over 8,000 miles into north-west China.

During China's struggle against Japan, Mao's communists and Chiang Kai-Shek's nationalists joined forces, but following the end of World War Two and the surrender of Japan, the two parties resumed a civil war that had originally started in 1927. Having finally defeated the Chinese nationalists, Chairman Mao proclaimed the People's Republic of China on 1 October 1949, with the words: 'The Chinese people have now stood up!'

Harry S. Truman 1884–1972

In January 1945 Truman was appointed US vice-president, but following Roosevelt's death eleven weeks later, found himself taking the leading role as the Second World War drew to a close. He remains the only person in history to authorize the use of atomic weapons, which, in August 1945, brought about Japan's surrender and the end of the war.

In March 1947, Truman articulated the need to alleviate poverty within Europe to prevent extreme ideologies taking root. 'The seeds of totalitarian regimes,' he said, 'are nurtured by misery and want.' In other words, communism appealed to those suffering from hardship. Remove the hardship and you remove the appeal of communism. In what became known as the 'Truman Doctrine', Truman believed that communism had to be contained, and that America could not, as it did after the First World War, turn its back on Europe – isolationism was no longer an option. In the post-war era a stable Europe and the future of the 'free world' was a necessity.

The Truman Doctrine initiated the European Recovery Program, more commonly known as the Marshall Plan, after its facilitator, George C. Marshall.

Truman also oversaw the successful Berlin Airlift and the formation of NATO but his later years in office were overshadowed by the Korean War.

Dwight D. Eisenhower 1890–1969

During the Second World War, Eisenhower, as supreme commander of Allied Forces, masterminded the D-Day landings in Normandy and the subsequent battle for France and push into Germany.

He was often resented for his lack of combat experience, but was known for his diplomacy, fostering a sense of collaboration between the British and Americans, and his ability to cope with conflicting egos.

After the war Eisenhower was feted by both the Republicans and Democrats but served in various non-political posts, culminating in his appointment as supreme commander of NATO. In 1952 he resigned from the army and entered politics as the Republican candidate for the presidency, winning the November 1952 election under the slogan 'I like Ike'. He brought about the end of the Korean War, and allowed Joseph McCarthy free rein in the anti-communist witch-hunts.

He was re-elected in 1956.

Nikita Khrushchev 1894–1971

A devoted servant of Stalin, Khrushchev survived the Great Purges and, having actively supported them, rose through the ranks of the Soviet hierarchy. Following Stalin's death in March 1953, Khrushchev emerged from the political manoeuvring within the Politburo to become Stalin's unlikely successor.

A Ukrainian peasant by origin, Khrushchev was impulsive, rotund, by turns vindictive and charming. During a UN meeting in New York in October 1960, Khrushchev famously protested about the proceedings by banging his shoe against his desk. But his 'different roads to socialism' meant an entirely new approach to leadership from that of his predecessor.

In February 1956, at the Soviet Twentieth Party Congress, in front of a gathering of the Kremlin hierarchy, Khrushchev delivered a four-hour speech in which he denounced Stalin's reign and his cult of personality whilst promising a degree of autonomy to the countries of the Eastern Bloc.

Khrushchev loved to travel. In September 1959, he visited the USA, and on a tour of the country, was impressed and intimidated in equal measure. Two months earlier, in an exchange with the US Vice-President, Richard Nixon, Khrushchev said, 'We [the Soviet Union] have existed not quite forty-two years but in another seven years we will be on the same level as America. When we catch you up, and in passing you by, we will wave to you.'

The Soviet Union's relations with China fared little better during Khrushchev's term in power. Chairman Mao viewed with growing disdain what he saw as the Soviet Union's co-existence with America. Khrushchev's withdrawal of missiles from Cuba was, to Mao, further evidence of his weakness.

Khrushchev dealt brusquely with the 1953 uprisings, first in Poland, then in Hungary; and in 1962 brought the world to the brink of nuclear war during the Cuban Missile Crisis.

Domestically, Khrushchev's attempts at introducing new initiatives, such as harvesting grain in Central Asia, backfired despite some initial success, leaving whole tracts of land useless.

In 1964, Khrushchev was deposed and immediately sidelined. Depressed and isolated, Khrushchev dictated his memoirs, which, although denounced by the Soviet Union, were published to much acclaim in the West. He died in 1971 but was denied a state funeral and a place of honour in the Kremlin Wall. His death was announced by *Pravda* with a single sentence.

John Fitzgerald Kennedy 1917–63

John Fitzgerald Kennedy graduated from college with the 'Most Likely to Succeed' prize. An energetic child and fond of practical jokes, Kennedy was nonetheless beset with ill health from an early age.

The son of the US ambassador to the UK, Kennedy was well travelled and was in London on the day Germany invaded Poland, thus triggering the Second World War. Kennedy wrote a book about Britain's policy regarding Hitler, *Why England Slept*, which became a bestseller.

Rejected by the US army because of his back pain, an ailment that would haunt him his whole life, Kennedy joined the navy in 1941, becoming an intelligence officer, and was later promoted to lieutenant in the Motor Torpedo Boat Squadron.

In August 1943, patrolling near the Solomon Islands in the South Pacific, Kennedy's boat was hit by a Japanese destroyer. Two of his men were killed outright but Kennedy and the six surviving crew members clung to the wreckage of the boat. Kennedy managed to get his men to safety, for which he earned a medal and high praise.

His older brother, Joseph Junior, was killed during the war in 1944.

In 1952, Kennedy was elected to the US Senate but his rise through the ranks of the Democratic Party was hampered by continuing back problems, with him twice needing major spinal surgery. On one occasion, he became so ill, Kennedy received the last rites. In 1956, whilst recovering from surgery, Kennedy wrote a biographical book about US senators, a publication that won him the 1957 Pulitzer Prize for Biography.

Aged forty-three, Kennedy became the youngest elected US president, when in November 1960 he defeated the future president, Richard Nixon, by a mere 0.3 per cent. He was also the first Roman Catholic to hold the post. He was popular and respected, his youth symbolizing a new, bright beginning within the free world.

However, in April 1961, a US-backed invasion of Cuba at the Bay of Pigs failed to raise a counter-uprising against the newly installed Marxist regime of Fidel Castro. Kennedy was heavily criticized but held his nerve during the subsequent Cuban Missile Crisis of 1962.

On 22 November 1963, whilst on the campaign trail in Dallas, Kennedy was assassinated.

Richard Nixon 1913–1994

As a Republican congressman, Richard Milhous Nixon made his name during the 1950s McCarthy era of communist witch-hunts, particularly in his rigorous prosecution of Alger Hiss, a high-ranking State Department official accused of passing information to the Soviets.

From 1953 to 1961 Nixon served as Dwight D. Eisenhower's vice-president, but allegations of financial irregularity almost finished his career and Nixon had to defend himself on television. At the time this was seen as a revolutionary use of this new medium. He survived and, in 1960, stood for president, narrowly losing to John F. Kennedy.

Failure two years later in his bid for governor of California marked the low point of Nixon's pre-presidential career. However, in November 1968, Nixon re-emerged and stood again for president, promising to 'bring us together', and pledging the withdrawal of troops from Vietnam. This time he was successful and, true to his promise, he gradually handed back the organization of the day-to-day military operations to the South Vietnamese in what he called a policy of 'Vietnamization'. Following the Paris Accords of January 1973, the last American soldiers had left Vietnam by the end of March.

Nixon advanced the Cold War period of détente, an acknowledgement of the differences between the East and the West and an attempt to make the world a more secure place. He exchanged visits with both China and the Soviet Union and oversaw the SALT agreements (Strategic Arms Limitation Talks).

Nixon was re-elected in 1972 in one of the largest landslide victories in US history. Within two years however, a failed burglary at the Democratic Party's HQ in the Watergate buildings in Washington DC started the process that would lead to Nixon's downfall. His attempts to conceal his involvement and tamper with evidence only damaged him further. Although Nixon claimed that he was 'not a crook', the Watergate prosecutor nonetheless found enough evidence to start the process of impeachment. On 8 August 1974, Nixon resigned, the only president in American history to do so.

His successor, Gerald Ford, unconditionally pardoned the disgraced ex-president. In reply, Nixon said, 'No words can describe the depths of my regret and pain at the anguish my mistakes over Watergate have caused the nation and the presidency, a nation I so deeply love and an institution I so greatly respect.'

He died from a stroke, aged eighty-one, on 22 April 1994.

John Paul II (Karol Wojtyla) 1920–2005

Karol Wojtyla experienced at first hand the German occupation of Poland during the Second World War. During the war, he worked as a stonecutter in a limestone quarry outside Krakow, followed by a stint in a chemical factory. The factory work, deemed essential by the Nazis, gave Wojtyla a work permit, which saved him from deportation. In August 1944 the Nazis initiated a round-up of able-bodied men and boys, but Wojtyla, hiding in the archbishop's palace, managed to avoid detection.

Wojtyla's mother died when he was eight years old, and his older brother four years later. His father, a lieutenant in the Polish army, died in February 1941. The grieving Wojtyla kept a vigil over his body the whole night. He was to say later, 'At twenty, I had already lost all the people I loved.'

Wojtyla was ordained as a priest in 1946 and appointed Archbishop of Krakow in 1967, often criticizing the communist regime of Poland. He was made a cardinal three years later and in 1978, following the death of Pope John Paul I, Wojtyla was elected pope as John Paul II, the first non-Italian to hold the post since 1522.

Known as the Travelling Pope, the energetic John Paul visited 129 countries during his pontificate, touring cities in his famous Popemobile. On his first visit home as pope, in June 1979, he fell to his feet and kissed the ground at Warsaw Airport.

On 13 May 1981, the pope survived an assassination attempt as he entered St Peter's Square in Rome. He recovered and during Christmas 1983 visited his would-be assassin in prison. Rumours persisted that the Soviet Union, threatened by the pope's support for Solidarity (Poland's independent trade union), was behind the attempt.

In his latter years, John Paul suffered from Parkinson's disease and he died on 2 April 2005. He had served for over twenty-six years, the second-longest pope. His funeral attracted the largest ever crowd for a funeral and the greatest number of heads of state in history, including nine monarchs and over seventy presidents. Mikhail Gorbachev said of Pope John Paul II, 'The collapse of the Iron Curtain would have been impossible without him.'

Pope John Paul II was beatified on 1 May 2011.

Ronald Reagan 1911–2004

Ronald Reagan worked as a baseball commentator before joining the US army reserve in 1937 as a second lieutenant. Whilst in the army, Reagan also started his film career, in which he became a successful B-movie actor, appearing in over twenty-five largely forgettable films during a period of twenty-five years up to 1964.

During the Second World War, Reagan's two careers coincided. His poor eyesight limited his options within the US military to mainly producing army training films.

In 1940, Reagan married the actress Jane Wyman, but the marriage ended and he remains the only US president to have been divorced. He remarried in 1952, this time to Nancy Davis.

Following the war and his discharge from the army, Reagan entered politics as a Democrat and a supporter of Harry S. Truman before changing his allegiance to the Republicans. In 1966, he was elected to serve as governor of California, a post he held for eight years.

In 1980, on the third time of trying, Reagan was nominated as the Republican presidential candidate and won the subsequent election, becoming the fortieth US president and, a few days short of his seventieth birthday, the oldest president in America's history.

In 1983 Reagan predicted: 'Communism is another sad, bizarre chapter in human history whose last pages even now are being written,' and that the 'forward march of freedom and democracy will leave Marxism-Leninism on the ash heap of history'. The 'Reagan Doctrine' provided support for anti-communist fighters throughout the world. In 1979 the Soviet Union invaded Afghanistan and Reagan provided the Mujahideen, fighting the Soviets, with cash, arms and training.

Reagan met several times with Soviet leader Mikhail Gorbachev and between them they ushered in a new period of rapprochement and greater understanding, which led, ultimately, to the ending of the Cold War.

In 1994, Reagan announced that he was suffering from Alzheimer's disease. He died ten years later, aged ninety-three, on 5 June 2004.

Mikhail Gorbachev 1931–

Mikhail Gorbachev's grandfather, a Communist Party member,

was caught up in Stalin's purges during the 1930s and, having been arrested by the NKVD, was tortured and imprisoned. But his grandfather never lost faith with the communist cause and introduced the young Gorbachev to the writings of Marx and Lenin.

During the Second World War, the family village was occupied by the invading Germans and Gorbachev later described the experience of war for his generation: 'It has burned us, leaving its mark both on our characters and in our view of the world.'

Gorbachev studied law and, on graduation, joined the Komsomol (the Communist Youth Organization). Over the next three decades he rose through the ranks of the party, sponsored by his mentor, Yuri Andropov.

Andropov succeeded Leonid Brezhnev as general secretary of the party in 1982 and Gorbachev was tipped to be his successor. But on Andropov's death in February 1984, the post fell, not to Gorbachev, but to the ageing Konstantin Chernenko. However, Gorbachev spread his influence so that when Chernenko died after only thirteen months as leader the post finally fell to him. Aged fifty-four, Gorbachev was the youngest general secretary in Soviet history, and the first to be born after the Russian Revolution of 1917.

His youth and progressive ideas alarmed the communist hardliners, whose fears were confirmed when Gorbachev ushered in a reformist programme, and introduced into the political lexicon the words *perestroika* (reconstruction) and *glasnost* (openness). The Soviet system's inept handling of the Chernobyl crisis highlighted the need for reform.

Immediately on coming to power, Gorbachev proposed a reduction in the number of nuclear arms held by the superpowers. In November 1985, Gorbachev met US president Ronald Reagan for the first time. Reagan, who had referred to the Soviet Union as the 'evil empire', was impressed by the new man in the Kremlin.

As general secretary, Gorbachev inherited the problem of Afghanistan where his predecessors had become embroiled in a lengthy war. Gorbachev hoped for a speedy conclusion to the conflict by committing greater numbers of troops. Although initially successful, Soviet forces were unable to maintain the momentum. The human cost was unacceptable to public opinion in the Soviet Union and ultimately Gorbachev had to agree, calling Afghanistan a 'bleeding wound'. The last Soviet troops withdrew on 15 February 1989.

Gorbachev will be remembered for his role during the Cold War. Through their several meetings, Reagan and Gorbachev helped ease international tension and, despite their ideological and cultural differences, the two men built a rapport that was to have a real and lasting effect on the ending of the Cold War.

Appendix Two:
Timeline of the Cold War

1940s

7 May 1945	Second World War: Germany surrenders.
14 August 1945	Second World War: Japan surrenders.
5 March 1946	Churchill's 'Iron Curtain' speech.
12 March 1947	Harry S. Truman proposes the 'Truman Doctrine'.
5 June 1947	Announcement of the Marshall Plan.
25 February 1948	Communist takeover in Czechoslovakia.
24 June 1948	Start of the Berlin Blockade.
4 April 1949	NATO established by Washington Treaty.
12 May 1949	End of the Berlin Blockade.
23 May 1949	Formal division into East and West Germany.
29 August 1949	Soviet Union detonates its first atomic bomb.
1 October 1949	People's Republic of China founded.

1950s

February 1950	Start of the McCarthy era.

25 June 1950	Start of the Korean War.
19 October 1950	China enters Korean War.
1 November 1952	USA detonates world's first hydrogen bomb.
5 March 1953	Death of Stalin.
16 June 1953	Uprising in East Germany.
27 July 1953	End of Korean War.
21 July 1954	Vietnam divided at the 17th parallel.
14 May 1955	Formation of the Warsaw Pact.
25 February 1956	Khrushchev denounces Stalin's method of rule.
June 1956	Polish Uprising.
23 October 1956	Start of Hungarian Uprising.
November 1956	Suez Crisis.
10 November 1956	End of the Hungarian Uprising.
4 October 1957	Soviet Union launches the first satellite, or Sputnik, into space.
January 1958	Chairman Mao launches the Great Leap Forward.
1 January 1959	Fidel Castro takes power in Cuba.
September 1959	Khrushchev visits USA.
26 September 1959	Start of Vietnam War.
1960s	
May 1960	US U-2 spy plane shot down over Moscow.
12 April 1961	Soviet cosmonaut, Yuri Gagarin, becomes the first man in space.
17 April 1961	US-backed Bay of Pigs invasion.
12–13 August 1961	Berlin Wall erected.
October 1962	Cuban Missile Crisis.

June 1963	John F. Kennedy visits West Berlin.
22 November 1963	Assassination of Kennedy.
2 August 1964	Gulf of Tonkin incident escalates Vietnam War.
16 May 1966	Chairman Mao launches the Cultural Revolution.
5–10 June 1967	Arab–Israeli Six-Day War.
4 April 1968	Assassination of Martin Luther King.
August 1968	Soviet tanks crush Czechoslovakian revolt.
20 July 1969	USA lands first man on the moon.
1970s	
February 1972	Richard Nixon visits China.
26 May 1972	SALT I signed.
15 January 1973	Nixon halts US bombing of North Vietnam.
30 April 1973	North Vietnamese tanks enter Saigon.
6–25 October 1973	Arab–Israeli Yom Kippur War.
8 August 1974	Nixon resigns following Watergate scandal.
30 April 1975	South Vietnam surrenders. End of war.
30 August 1975	Helsinki Accords signed.
16 October 1978	Karol Wojtyla appointed Pope John Paul II.
1 April 1979	Islamic republic proclaimed in Iran.
24 December 1979	Soviet Union's invasion of Afghanistan.

1980s

13 December 1981	Martial law imposed in Poland and Solidarity banned.
1 September 1983	Soviet fighter plane shoots down a Korean civilian airliner.
26 April 1986	Explosion at nuclear power plant at Chernobyl.
12 June 1987	Ronald Reagan visits West Berlin.
15 May 1988	Soviet troops start to withdraw from Afghanistan.
15 February 1989	Soviet withdrawal completed.
16 June 1989	Reburial and state funeral of Imre Nagy.
June 1989	Student uprising in Beijing.
24 August 1989	First post-war, non-communist eastern European government comes to power in Poland.
7 October 1989	East Germany celebrates fortieth anniversary.
9 November 1989	Fall of the Berlin Wall.
17 November 1989	Start of the Velvet Revolution in Czechoslovakia.
25 December 1989	Execution of Nicolae and Elena Ceauşescu in Romania.

1990s

11 March–4 May 1990	Baltic States declare independence.
3 October 1990	Germany reunified.
12 June 1991	Boris Yeltsin elected president of the Russian Federation.
June 1991	Last Soviet tanks leave eastern Europe.

1 July 1991	Warsaw Pact dissolved.
19 August 1991	Failed communist coup in Russia.
8 December 1991	Founding of the Commonwealth of Independent States (CIS).
25 December 1991	Gorbachev resigns.
31 December 1991	USSR formally dissolved.

Got Another Hour?

History in an Hour is a series of eBooks to help the reader learn the basic facts of a given subject area. Everything you need to know is presented in a straightforward narrative and in chronological order. No embedded links to divert your attention, nor a daunting book of 600 pages with a 35-page introduction. Just straight in, to the point, sixty minutes, done. Then, having absorbed the basics, you may feel inspired to explore further. Give yourself sixty minutes and see what you can learn…

To find out more visit http://historyinanhour.com or follow us on twitter: http://twitter.com/historyinanhour

1066: History in an Hour by Kaye Jones

Covering the major events of the year 1066, this is a clear account of England's political turmoil during which the country had three different kings and fought three large-scale battles in defence of the kingdom, including the infamous Battle of Hastings.

The Afghan Wars: History in an Hour by Rupert Colley

A comprehensive overview of the wars that have been fought in Afghanistan for almost four decades, including the politics of the Taliban, why Osama Bin Laden was so significant, and why it is still so hard to achieve peace in the country.

The American Civil War: History in an Hour by Kat Smutz

A clear account of the politics and major turning points of the war that split the country in half as the northern and southern states fought over the right to keep slaves, changing American culture forever.

American Slavery: History in an Hour by Kat Smutz

A broad overview of the major events in the history of American slavery, detailing the arrival of the first slaves, the Southern plantations, the Civil War, and the historical and cultural legacy of slavery in the United States.

Ancient Egypt: History in an Hour by Anthony Holmes

A succinct exploration of the historic rise of Egyptian civilisation and its influence on the world, covering Egyptian gods, mummification and burial rituals, and the Pyramids of Giza.

Black History: History in an Hour by Rupert Colley

A clear overview of the long and varied history of African Americans, including everything from slavery, the Civil War and emancipation to the civil rights movement and the Black Panther Party.

Dickens: History in an Hour by Kaye Jones

A comprehensive overview of the life of arguably Britain's most successful and beloved writer, including the poverty of his childhood, the evolution of his novels, his tours of Europe and America, and his occasionally scandalous private life.

George Washington: History in an Hour by David B. McCoy

The essential chronicle of George Washington's life, from his middle-class Virginian upbringing to his unanimous election as America's first president, and the prominent role he played in shaping America as we know it today.

The Gunpowder Plot: History in an Hour by Sinead Fitzgibbon

An engaging account of the infamous plot by a group of Catholic traitors, led by Guy Fawkes, to blow up the Houses of Parliament and James I, including details of the motives behind their drastic actions and how the plot came to be discovered.

Henry VIII's Wives: History in an Hour by Julie Wheeler

An inclusive introduction to the six diverse personalities of Henry VIII's wives, the events that led them to their individual fates, and the different impacts they each had on King and country.

Hitler: History in an Hour by Rupert Colley

A coherent overview of Hitler's early life, service in World War I, rise to the top of the Nazi Party and eventually the head of state, covering all the key moments of the dictator's life through to his death and the crumbling of his empire.

JFK: History in an Hour by Sinead Fitzgibbon

A comprehensive insight into the life of America's youngest elected president, assassinated barely one thousand days into his presidency, examining his navigation of the Space Race, his sympathies with the civil rights movement, and the chronic illness that affected him throughout his life.

The Medieval Anarchy: History in an Hour by Kaye Jones

A look at the unprecedented chaos and disorder that followed the death of King Henry I, leading to England's first, and often forgotten, civil war, as well as an overview of the plots and violence that ensued during this nineteen-year bloody conflict.

Nazi Germany: History in an Hour by Rupert Colley

A concise explanation which covers the major events behind the Nazi Party's climb to power, what it was like to live in Nazi Germany, and how Hitler brought the world into war.

The Queen: History in an Hour by Sinead Fitzgibbon

A compelling history of the UK's second-longest-reigning

monarch, covering her 1953 coronation to her Diamond Jubilee in 2012 and examining her long reign, during which the British Empire has transformed.

The Reformation: History in an Hour by Edward A. Gosselin

A concise look at the spread of religious dissidence across Europe in the sixteenth century, including the events that caused people to question the ideas of the established Catholic Church and the resulting wars, migration and disunity.

The Russian Revolution: History in an Hour by Rupert Colley

Covering all the major events in a straightforward overview of the greatest political experiment ever conducted, and how it continues to influence both Eastern and Western politics today.

The Siege of Leningrad: History in an Hour by Rupert Colley

A broad account of one of the longest sieges in history in which over the course of 900 days the city of Leningrad resisted German invasion, contributing to the defeat of the Nazis at the cost of over one million civilian lives.

South Africa: History in an Hour by Anthony Holmes

A fascinating overview of South Africa's history of oppression and racial inequality and how after years of violence and apartheid, Nelson Mandela, the country's first black President, led the country to unite and become the 'Rainbow Nation'.

Stalin: History in an Hour by Rupert Colley

A succinct exploration of Joseph Stalin's long leadership of the Soviet Union, covering his rise to power, his role in the Russian Revolution, and his terrifying regime that directly and negatively affected the lives of so many.

Titanic: History in an Hour by Sinead Fitzgibbon

An account of the catastrophe, including the failures of the White Star Line, the significance of class and the legacy of the disaster in Britain and America.

The Vietnam War: History in an Hour by Neil Smith

A clear account of the key events of the most important Cold War-era conflict, including the circumstances leading up to the Vietnam War, the deadly guerrilla warfare, the fall of Saigon and the backlash of anti-war protests in America.

World War One: History in an Hour by Rupert Colley

A clear overview of the road to war, the major turning points and battles, and the key leaders involved, as well as the lasting impact the Great War had on almost every country in the world.

World War Two: History in an Hour by Rupert Colley

Covering the major events in a broad overview of the politics and violence of the most devastating conflict the world has ever seen, and how it changed the world in unimaginable ways.